Chakras

Introductory Courses On Chakra And Reiki Healing,
Buddhism, And Third Eye Awakening

*(Discover How To Enhance Physical Well-being And
Enhance Cognitive Abilities Through The Utilization Of
Kundalini Energy)*

Jordon Matthews

TABLE OF CONTENT

Anahata: Foundation and Healing 1

Common Errors in Attempting to Heal the Heart Chakra...15

Anahata (heart chakra) 23

Anahata is the Heart Chakra............................62

Solar Plexus Chakra is the third chakra.....................71

Chakra of the Soul Star 97

Self-Talk That Is Negative............................106

Mudra Related to the Third Eye Chakra..................119

As a Spiritual Practice, Sensuality..............................131

Effects of Chakra Blockage or Imbalance................147

Anahata: Foundation and Healing

Chakra, the number four The location is at the center of the chest.

The heart, upper back with ribcage and thoracic cavity, lower lungs, blood and circulatory system, and skin are all body correspondences.

The thymus is the corresponding gland. The thymus gland governs growth and the lymphatic system. It is also responsible for activating and strengthening the immune system.

Sensory Abilities: Touch

A lotus with twelve petals is the symbol.

Mantra: Yam Element: Air

Venus is the planet.

As we've just discovered, mending the solar plexus leads to identifying your innermost defects. While working on your self-confidence might help you heal these flaws, true self-acceptance also necessitates self-love. The heart chakra, also known as Anahata, is the chakra of self-love, which is important in integrating the Shadow. In truth, shadow work is only feasible when we love and accept ourselves. We must also forgive those who have injured us and contributed to the formation of our Shadow. So, are you prepared? Let's look at the heart chakra's significance, its critical role, and how you may promote its healing.

The Chakra of the Heart: The Most Important Factors

To begin, the heart chakra is located in the center of the seven-chakra system, acting as a link between the earthy concerns of the lower chakras and the more spiritual qualities of the upper chakras. It assists you in finding balance by recognizing that both sides are necessary for your well-being.

Furthermore, as the name implies, the heart chakra governs all types of love and relationships, including partnerships, friendships, and ties with family members. A healthy heart chakra allows us to maintain these connections and set boundaries that keep destructive dynamics at bay.

Genuine unconditional love is neither harmful nor selfish. Unconditional love means loving someone despite their flaws or mistakes in the past, seeing them for who they truly are, and choosing to love them nevertheless. It is a love that does not demand anything in return. While not without difficulties, unconditional love is founded on healthy and respectful relations. The heart chakra must be totally opened to love and connect with someone on such a profound level.

Another important factor in developing deep ties with others is trust. It can be lost for legitimate reasons like betrayal or infidelity. However, past events or negative cultural views can have an impact on one's ability to trust. The heart chakra teaches us the value of trust in healthy relationships and gives us insight into who we can trust and who shouldn't.

Forgiveness is also inextricably linked to trust. It is normal to hold onto your rage and judgment endlessly when someone wrongs you. Clinging to pain, on the other hand, will only make things worse. The heart chakra promotes a shift in perspective, allowing us to let go of judgment and finally forgive.

However, we must not overlook the necessity of loving oneself when discussing love. A balanced heart chakra allows you to love and embrace your inner self while acknowledging and embracing your imperfections. This quality, in particular, is essential for complete healing and integration of the Shadow.

Heart Chakra Blockages: Common Causes

It's no wonder many people today have blockages in their heart chakras, particularly regarding self-love.

Despite increased knowledge, the necessity of loving others has historically received far more focus, continuing a circle of suffering. So, let's look at some of the most common causes of a blocked heart chakra.

Shame: Shame, a common issue in chakra blockages, significantly impacts our ability to love ourselves. Experiences of being shamed by others might leave you with deep-seated thoughts that you are unlovable or undeserving of a loving relationship. So, among many other issues, shame maintains obstructions in the heart chakra.

Rejection: In personal relationships or other circumstances, rejection may be extremely unpleasant and harmful to our sense of self-worth. Even respectful rejections can cause feelings of unlovability and develop blockages in the heart chakra, making giving and receiving love difficult.

Betrayal is a highly upsetting and heartbreaking experience. Whether it's discovering that our spouse is having an affair or being duped by a close friend, betrayal destroys our faith in others and makes it difficult to open our hearts again or feel deserving of love. Fear of potential betrayal and the emotional agony that comes with it contribute to heart chakra blockages.

Abuse: It is impossible to overestimate the negative consequences of abuse on mental health and the energy system. Abuse shatters our sense of self and erodes our self-esteem and trust in others. Abusers' fear typically lingers, making it difficult to open the heart chakra and believe in the potential of genuine love and connection. The guilt induced by abusers impedes self-love even more and might contribute to a blocked heart chakra.

Grief: Losing a loved one is a heartbreaking event. As a preventive precaution against future grief, deep loss, and the following grieving process can lead the heart chakra to shut down. For some, grief lingers, causing a protracted obstruction that impedes emotional healing.

Indications of Heart Chakra Issues

Heart Chakra Discord

A heart chakra imbalance can show in a variety of ways. For example, you may have a propensity to give and be there for others but not receive affection in return. Deep down, you may secretly wish for praise and affirmation for your acts of love, and it can be upsetting when your efforts go unnoticed. Alternatively, you may represent strength and support to others while finding it difficult to accept and be open to receiving love. Tenderness and kindness may perplex you, and you may tell yourself that you do not require affection from others. This position is frequently accompanied by a "proud" manner, indicating inner defense mechanisms and resistance to emotional anguish and vulnerability.

Heart Chakra Blockage:

A malfunctioning heart chakra might make you feel vulnerable and reliant on the affection and sympathy of others. Rejection has a profound effect on you, causing you to withdraw into your shell and experience melancholy and depression.

Although you want to provide love, your fear of being rejected again prevents you from doing so, increasing your sense of inadequacy. Perhaps you try to compensate for a lack of love by being extremely nice and accommodating, bringing joy to everyone equally but not allowing yourself to build deeper ties. However, when genuinely expressing your heart, you may resist it for fear of being wounded. When the heart chakra is entirely closed, emotional dryness and apathy appear. You need powerful external stimuli to feel anything, and you have emotional imbalances and may even be depressed.

Watch out for these warning signs:

Feeling inadequate or having low self-esteem.

Shyness and feeling uneasy in social circumstances.

Isolation and disconnection from others.

Social interactions and antisocial behavior are avoided.

When alone, one experiences intense fear or discomfort.

Feelings of melancholy, hopelessness, or depression that persist.

Difficulty establishing and maintaining romantic relationships.

Anxiety.

Narcissism.

Empathy is lacking.

A weaker immune system, resulting in recurrent infections, is a red flag.

Asthma and recurrent bronchitis are examples of respiratory issues.

Cardiovascular issues and heart-related diseases.

Problems with circulation.

Thymus gland dysfunction or imbalance influences the immune system.

These signs and symptoms point to an imbalanced heart chakra and emphasize the significance of treating and mending this energy center to restore emotional well-being and harmony. Remember that the above symptoms might vary in severity and may be impacted by personal circumstances. If you have many physical symptoms or recurring issues, don't hesitate to contact your doctor or a mental health expert.

Common Errors in Attempting to Heal the Heart Chakra

Before we get into the Shadow parts of the heart chakra, I want you to be aware of several typical mistakes people make while attempting to cure this chakra:

Resentment and resentment: The heart chakra is about forgiving and letting go. Holding on to bitterness, grudges, or past injuries can also hinder healing. So, to discharge emotional baggage, encourage healing, and strive to practice forgiveness towards others and oneself.

Lack of Self-Love: As we've seen, the heart chakra is also about self-love and acceptance. Neglecting self-care and engaging in self-criticism or lack of self-compassion can particularly damage this chakra's healing. So foster self-love, engage in self-care rituals, and always treat yourself with kindness and compassion.

Unhealthy Boundaries: The heart chakra is all about interpersonal harmony and setting healthy boundaries. Healing will be hampered if you have weak boundaries or allow others to take advantage of you frequently. This is why you should always express your wants and respect the boundaries of others.

Closedness to Receiving and Giving Love: You should already know that the heart chakra is primarily concerned with giving and receiving love. Healing will be nearly impossible if you are closed off to love or have trouble accepting love from others. As a result, be open to accepting and freely expressing love, establishing meaningful connections and acts of compassion.

Healing and Vulnerability: The heart chakra also deals with healing and vulnerability. Heart chakra healing can be hampered by resisting the healing process or avoiding vulnerability. This is why you should be willing to embrace the therapeutic process and be vulnerable in safe and supportive places.

The Heart Chakra's Shadow Aspects

The appearance of the Shadow in the heart chakra can significantly impact our relationships with others and with ourselves. Self-love suffers when the heart chakra is blocked, causing us to engage in compensatory behaviors in our interactions. The Shadow can appear in a variety of ways through the heart chakra.

To begin with, people with heart chakra blockages frequently experience intense and overwhelming emotions due to unresolved concerns. Unfortunately, they may be unaware of their emotional difficulties, causing them to project their pain onto others.

This chakra, for example, is frequently a growing place for grudges and thoughts of hatred. These could be the result of generating sentiments of poor self-esteem. Inadequacy and unworthiness, for example, might encourage people to reroute their suffering by holding anger and casting judgment on others rather than addressing their healing.

Without self-esteem and self-love, some people seek emotional fulfillment from outside sources. They feel that specific friendships or partnerships will fill the void left by their loneliness and anguish. This distorted view of love depicts possible partners as instruments for their healing rather than as independent people to adore and love. Such destructive concepts of love rarely result in meaningful interactions, but societal forces continue to promote these beliefs. Furthermore, when people lack self-esteem, they become too needy and reliant on their spouses. This conduct might be characterized by a view that love should center around their personal needs, causing these relationships to thrive on emotional instability and drama.

We must also emphasize that many people turn to substance misuse to alleviate the agony caused by a closed-off heart chakra.

They are unable to face the need for personal healing because of this deceitful coping technique. Addiction, on the other hand, aggravates the suffering and magnifies other Shadow behaviors linked with a blocked heart chakra.

Understanding the relationship between the heart chakra and the Shadow is critical for emphasizing self-love and forgiveness during healing. True self-healing is difficult unless we accept and cherish our defects and blind spots. Furthermore, forgiveness must be extended to those who may have contributed to our difficulties, acknowledging that they, too, were operating from their own Shadows. While repairing the heart chakra may be a good place to start for some, it is critical to also open the lower chakras to get the necessary energy for overall healing. However, while I recommend starting with the root chakra, you can follow your instincts and focus on another chakra if desired.

Anahata (heart chakra)

Allow for the presence of love and light in your life. The heart chakra, also known as the Anahata chakra, is associated with feelings of love and compassion. It is the fourth energy point in your chest, located in the heart area and extending to the base of your throat, finishing below your breastbone. On the other hand, pink can be utilized to promote feelings of self-love and self-compassion. You will experience joy, compassion, peace, and tranquillity when your heart is open and flowing with love. Kindness to yourself, others, and all living beings on Earth will increase your heart core.

During meditation, you can also consciously expand your heart center to encompass the entire Universe and cosmos by seeing a green light beaming from your heart. Green is also the color of nature, so if you want to enrich your life with more love, incorporate more green into it. You can start spreading love to every cell in your body and everyone who crosses your way by placing beautiful plants in your house and office. This will significantly raise your vibration of love and strengthen feelings of kinship with others. Maintaining an open heart should be a priority since it affects your relationship throughout your life.

Put yourself first in your life. The more you show yourself love, compassion, and kindness, the better you will feel. It will naturally spread to others. This is the time when we improve our lives and become more influential. We make a difference in the world when we are kind, empathetic, and friendly to others. Everyone faces some form of difficult challenge in their life; thus, extending your heart chakra via acts of compassion will also have a good impact on the lives of others. This does not indicate that you must tolerate bad treatment or relationships of poor quality; rather, it implies that you simply extend love to everyone in general, and you can still set boundaries and trust your instincts about individuals who may not be a good company to maintain.

When it comes to healing and change, your most beloved connections should be your priority, and you can accomplish higher-quality relationships when your heart chakra is balanced, open, and flowing more with universal love. The celestial world is one of peace and love, whereas the terrestrial world is one of conflict and difficulty. This vortex of energy emitted by the Anahata can bring more harmony to your life by bridging the gap between the two worlds, allowing you to feel greater harmony and tranquility on Earth.

The Anahata chakra is also concerned with love, relationships, and conflict. You will feel intense emotional anguish in this location when you have conflict. It closes until you can transcend the difficulties that impede love from flowing more freely. Avoid burdening your heart or yourself by leaving unsolved problems or allowing strong emotions like anger and hatred to linger. Even though heart issues might be difficult to overcome, take time to develop healing thoughts and love, beginning by being nice to yourself and prioritizing your needs. That is usually a good place to begin.

An underactive heart chakra will result in more conflict and arguments. Still, an open and flowing heart chakra will result in reconciliation, trust building, and being more receptive to seeing another's point of view. Place your hands on your heart at any time of day and visualize a pure green light of love flowing and expanding in your heart center and all around you until it reaches the entire Earth, then the entire cosmos. Send love and peace to all living things, and let go of old grudges. Check in with yourself regularly, and if you experience pangs of emotional agony in your heart, try to resolve them or release them to the Universe for the ultimate healing.

Consider universal love as a magnificent green fountain of care and compassion pouring through you. Allow its wisdom and warmth to wash away the years' worth of grief. Declare aloud that it is time for renewal and transformation and that you are always deserving and worthy of love no matter what you did or did not do in the past. It's true: you've always deserved love; therefore, start feeling more deserving and chanting "yam" while meditating on your heart chakra.

Unblocking Your Heart Chakra

Use sandalwood, rose, lavender, or jasmine perfumes to focus on your heart center, opening yourself up to greater love, compassion, and joy in your life.

Say to yourself frequently that you believe in love, encourage more love into your life, and commit to loving yourself and others more and doing more of what you enjoy and dislike.

Activate your heart chakra by moving your body into heart-opening yoga poses. Bridge, upward-facing dog, sun salutations, and camel pose all open the chest. Choose yoga poses that open up the chest area.

Rose quartz, jade, green tourmaline, and aventurine crystals will attract more love and vibrate at a healing frequency to open the heart. Carry some with you, leave some around the house or in plants, and wear some as jewelry.

You can use sound meditation, words, or sentences to open the heart.

The Chakra of the Throat (Vishuddha)

which means "especially pure." It is associated with blue and is closely related to your heart chakra. Speaking your truth confidently from the heart will open this chakra and alleviate any tension that has built up due to previous "withholds" that you have experienced. This chakra influences both vocal and written communication. This chakra may become overactive if you are prevented from expressing yourself and your actual sentiments. This means you will have to raise your voice at times to be heard. Or it could become inactive, so you will avoid interacting out of fear and hurt.

Blue is also a thought-provoking color that stimulates self-expression. Knowledge is essential for personal and professional empowerment, making self-expression even more crucial for experiencing success and personal fulfillment. Through meditation and healing, try to connect with your throat chakra more often. The more you connect to the heart chakra, the more successful you will be in communicating from the heart. Avoid restricting your expression because you fear rejection or not gaining acceptance or love from others. Everything that becomes trapped inside us is bound to explode to restore the chakra to a healthy state of equilibrium. An unbalanced throat chakra can result in poor communication abilities, which will cause you much aggravation. Visualize a large blue ocean opening out to you regularly as you immerse yourself in its secrets, knowledge, and power. Simultaneously, imagine your expression is as passionate, confident, real, and captivating as the blue ocean. Chant the Sanskrit word "ham" as you do this to open up this chakra (Sahu, 2020).

This becomes clearer when we consider that our bodies only work the way they do because our cells constantly exchange information—in continual communication.

Thus far, so good. But it is one of Nonviolent Communication's key models, which was developed to understand how misconceptions or disputes in communication originate in the first place, that intrigues me the most about this. This is the concept of needs and tactics.

It's fairly simple: Everything we do and say stems from a desire to satisfy one of our basic needs. A need, such as freedom, security, nourishment, intimacy, involvement, or peace, is always positive in and of itself. However, we employ distinct, individual techniques to meet a need.

Most of the time, the tactics we employ to meet certain demands are influenced by what we learned in our family or environment—they are conditioned, and frequently at least largely unconscious, response patterns. And these techniques can be harmful to both others and ourselves.

Consider what human civilization's essentially beneficial urge to defend itself against flooding has done to rivers and their animal and plant inhabitants in many parts of Europe and the world.

The major method of society to meet its demand for security in this field, as is well known, is the construction of dams, canals, river diversions, and similar structural solutions, which in most cases adversely alter the natural equilibrium of these zones.

As a result, our requirements are always good and authentic. Our strategies, on the other hand, may have unintended repercussions. The better we understand our needs, the easier it will be to find other, non-harmful ways to meet them.

◆◆◆

◆◆◆

The association of the 'observer' with the 'thinking machine' processes causes suffering or frustration.

◆◆◆

What does this reveal about our personalities? First and foremost, consider the following:

Our thinking mind frequently pulls us out of the present moment. It plans, recalls, and compares future circumstances to fictitious goals and beliefs about how things should progress, and so on. So far, it is so good because that is what it should do.

The identification of us—the "observer"—with these projections of manas, our thinking machine, is what causes misery, or at least discomfort.

The biggest value of meditation is that it repeatedly brings us back to the present moment, exposing this identification as at least partially illusory and, therefore, putting everything into perspective.

So, what exactly does being in the present moment imply? Answering this question is far more complicated and intricate than one might expect. Wonderful teachers and authors such as Eckhart Tolle and Jon Kabat-Zinn, to mention a few, have provided excellent practical and philosophical answers.

But, to truly incorporate these insights into our lives, with all of the delights they provide, we must first understand and experience this state for ourselves. It is not enough to simply have heard about it.

We run the risk of getting lost in trivial details if we rely just on theory. For instance, which religion or meditation approach is the "right"? This isn't only a Western phenomenon; it happens whenever abstract concepts are discussed. Years ago, I was astonished to learn that even followers of some Buddhist schools disagree about who has the "right" intellectual understanding of emptiness and non-duality.

A deeper analysis of our philosophy is highly beneficial in avoiding being mired in unessential conceptual ideas while interpreting our meditation experiences, as revealed in Chapter 2.

On the one hand, this is necessary for the coherence of our emotional and mental worlds. Conversely, this is the only way to truly integrate the experience into our daily lives and use it to improve ourselves and the world.

Healing of the Third Eye Chakra

Changes in Lifestyle

Don't restrict yourself.

The third eye chakra opens up a world of possibilities for you. It offers millions of opportunities for you to accomplish the same thing. It allows you to see things in a new light. If you start limiting yourself and questioning everything you do, you may place unnecessary strain on this chakra. Begin to think more boldly. Don't consider it from a narrow perspective. Think in increasingly broad strokes. Don't just consider yourself; consider the broader welfare as well. Expanding your mental horizons can help you deal with the challenges in this chakra.

Work on brain balancing.

The third eye chakra is linked to your brain and mental abilities. When the third eye chakra is functioning, channeling the energy takes a lot of effort. To sharpen your mind, you must engage in brain-balancing exercises.

Concentrate on your root chakra.

Keeping your root chakra healthy is essential for bringing your third eye chakra into equilibrium. This chakra can blur the gap between reality and fantasy. You can begin to imagine the impossible. You may lose your sense of reality and begin formulating unachievable goals. If your root chakra weakens, you may struggle with the forces around you. To keep your third eye chakra balanced, you must also keep your root chakra steady and functional.

Don't rely on your imagination.

At times, the third eye chakra can cause delusions. People begin to live in an imaginary world when unprepared to deal with energy of this size. Your mind and body should be prepared to deal with these high-intensity points. You should quit daydreaming and start living your life.

Keep an eye out for unfavorable influences.

The third eye chakra broadens your perception. This implies you begin to sense the presence of various energies around you. You start interacting with them more often. Those energies may impact you if your energy field is weak or your root chakra is weak. When your third eye chakra is out of harmony, you must be cautious of the people and energy you interact with. It would be beneficial if you immediately began working on boosting your energy field.

Indigo

THIS CHAKRA'S COLOR IS INDIGO, AND IT WOULD BE HELPFUL IF YOU COULD KEEP THINGS OF THIS COLOR AROUND YOU TO HELP STRENGTHEN YOUR ENERGY FIELD.

Yoga postures

There is no particular yoga that is especially beneficial in developing this chakra. Concentrating on improving your consciousness level as much as possible would be beneficial. This chakra is linked to intellectual and spiritual realization rather than physical manifestations. Make an effort to increase your concentration.

Meditation

Specific third-eye chakra meditations can help you balance this chakra. It would be beneficial to limit the influence of negative energies surrounding you when you sit for meditation, as your energy field can sometimes become weak. Even if bad ideas arise when meditating, you must not be afraid.

Crystals

This chakra can be balanced and healed using lepidolite, sugilite, lapis lazuli, amethyst, fluorite, tanzanite, clear quartz, star sapphire, and kyanite.

Aromatherapy Oils

This chakra can be balanced using frankincense, lavender, and sandalwood.

Crown Chakra Rejuvenation

Changes in Lifestyle

- Be respectful to your elders.

This is the highest chakra, and it is related to spiritual awareness. If this chakra remains balanced, you will be highly regarded, have a healing touch, and be wise. You would constantly be in the best of moods. It's like being euphoric all the time, regardless of what's going on around you. However, if this chakra fails, it might be frustrating. Respect for others, especially seniors, is the best method to balance this chakra. It fills you with humility to show respect to your elders. This prevents the accumulation of negative energy.

- Be grateful

Be grateful for everything in life. Don't be grumpy or depressed. The happier you are, the more balanced the energy in this chakra will be.

- Be more charitable.

The more you give to others, the more love and respect you will receive. Regarding spiritual consciousness, whatever you give away is the true wealth you may achieve. As a result, it is critical to continue participating in philanthropic activities.

Just a few physical methods and equipment for balancing or healing this chakra. This chakra is almost external to your body and is not influenced by material objects. Yoga and meditation are the best ways to keep this chakra balanced. Both of these exercises can aid in the health and balance of this chakra.

Meditation Techniques for Opening the Third Eye

According to the previous section, the third eye is above the brows. It is one in charge of visual abilities, such as perceiving visions, flashes, and symbols. Meditation is an important practice for increasing the potency of your clairvoyance talents. Aside from meditation, you must concentrate on your third eye to trust your external experiences and ensure that your third eye is open if it is closed.

It may not open immediately; you must ask it to spread until it does. When it opens, you will experience a sense of serenity and warmth throughout your body. The opening of the obstructed bodily component will cause the sensation. It must be awake for everything to work well.

You must be preoccupied with a superb approach for your close to open the third eye. It is necessary because it is an ethereal bridge connecting the physical and spiritual realms. The soul makes you unique and alive, and you must gain access to it through the third eye-opening. It will help you get more knowledge and appreciate your experiences more. The third eye does not work alone but in conjunction with the hypothalamus gland. That is, it will affect some of your key biological activities.

Opening your third eye allows you to access the wisdom contained in your soul. You will surely have the best spiritual guide when you meditate to open your third eye. A powerful awakening will occur, and you will recognize the talent within you that is about to carry you to higher spiritual levels. You can choose to awaken your third eye through meditation. It can be done independently or with the assistance of an expert. The expert will assist you through simple measures to ensure your eye is open during the guided meditation. Some of the strategies include, but are not limited to:

Step 1: Select a Location

To achieve the fundamental goal of meditation, you must seek out a location with few distractions. To begin, all you need is a calm area. When selecting a site, make certain that you will be consistent. The individual who will lead you in meditation should be compatible with you. Your body and mind must adjust to the new environment. You should assign someone to be in charge of activating your third eye. This is something else to think about when deciding on a site.

Step 2: Select a Time with Intention

After completing the first step, go to the second by deciding when you will attend the guided meditation sessions. To be effective, you must attend the seminars daily. You should schedule the sessions at an appropriate time. It would be beneficial if you remained fixed at the moment you specified. Consider the time that will be most convenient for you, and your body and mind should be free and calm. You should avoid arranging the sessions right before or after your meals. A morning will be the most convenient for you. However, this does not preclude any other time from being appropriate. Consistency is required when choosing a time other than the morning.

Step 3: Stretch Before Beginning the Meditation Session

You should stretch before the meeting because you will be sitting longer. You can unwind by meditating on opening your third eye and recognizing your power. For at least a minute, try bending over and touching your toes. You can relax by stretching your arms above your head. Don't forget to lie on your back and ensure your feet are 90 degrees off the ground.

Step 4: Take a Position

Meditation cannot be practiced while standing. Sitting in a relaxed position with your legs crossed would be beneficial. If you find this posture unpleasant and uncomfortable, change to a more comfortable one. You should choose a position that allows you to relax and focus swiftly on your breathing and meditation. It would be beneficial to sit on the floor with your legs crossed to better contemplate activating your third eye and accessing the hidden spiritual treasures. Open your chest and keep your back straight. Consider putting your hands on your knees or lap, depending on your posture. To enter the world of meditation, your head should be erect and closed, and your eyes should be lightly closed.

Step 5: Unwind.

After you've settled into a comfortable posture, the next natural step is to give your body time to adjust. When you are not relaxed, you cannot meditate. Be aware of how your body is feeling, and if there are any feelings you need to work with before the meditation, do so. Ascertain that your entire body is relaxed and prepared to begin the session. As you sit and relax, pay attention to each body component individually. Remove your focus from worries and prepare to give attention to the current moment. Make sure to feel your body expanding and contracting as you breathe in and out with each breath.

Step 6: Take a deep breath.

Breathing is an important meditation technique. Concentrate on how you breathe in and out and give your complete attention to living. Take deep breaths on the count of three as you inhale and exhale occasionally.

Step 7: Clear Your Mind

At this time, you will concentrate on the third eye, located in the center of your forehead. Your eyes are closed while you are still; transfer your gaze to the third eye. Concentrating without changing your gaze throughout the meditation procedure would be beneficial. Keep the attention; count backward from one hundred, but don't worry if you don't experience the third eye then. It may take some time to adjust to the meditation technique. It may take longer to activate your third eye, so don't be concerned. You must stay consistent; everything will fall into place over time.

Step 8: Unlock the Third Eye

When you've finished counting from a hundred backward, it's time to try to access the sight. Make sure you focus on the previous steps so that this point goes well. When you pay attention, you will see that everything but your third eye is dark. When the vision is engaged, your brain relaxes and functions completely differently. You will feel the energy surrounding you as both sides of your brain function in sync. You will notice a surge of energy coursing through your body and surrounding you. That is when you will realize you have gained access to your third eye. You know you are accessing the eye when you focus strongly on an object or image. For something to happen, the creature or thought must completely engulf your mind.

Step 9: Practice Using Your Third Eye

Everyone reacts differently to the activation of their third eye. You might have flashing visual effects in your thoughts and other sensations and images. If they can be laid out, it can be a way of viewing how your thoughts appear. You will gradually work on opening the eye as you focus on feeling your third eye.

Step 10: Maintain Your Concentration on the Third Eye

Concentrating on the third eye for ten to fifteen minutes would be beneficial. You may experience a headache during your first sessions, although this is common for practically every newcomer. There is no need to be concerned because the headache will disappear as you become accustomed to the practice. You must practice fully appreciating your third eye and focusing on a single vision. Pay close attention to the image you select among the ones that will emerge in your head. Make an effort to keep your attention focused on the choice you've made. When you focus on the third eye, it will gently open. That indicates you accomplished your goal when you chose to meditate. Your third eye will open, and you will have a wonderful experience with the priceless gift that you have within you.

Step 11: Exit Meditation Slowly

After completing your goal, the following step is to come out of the meditation. Remove your concentration from your third eye progressively while maintaining your relaxed state throughout the procedure. Your guide will advise you to be mindful of your breathing. When removing your thoughts from the meditation, you can count on focusing on your breathing. Slowly open your eyes to bring the process to a close.

If you need to open your third eye at any other moment, repeat the instructions above, and it will be much easier this time. This is because it will not be the first time. Work on making your body feel better and connecting with your inner self. However, this will not happen immediately because you must practice meditation before ascending to greater heights. You'll be more in tune with yourself and the energy surrounding you. That is the fundamental purpose of meditating to open your third eye.

You will see indications that your eye is open. You will no longer have self-doubt after you have opened the third eye. You will want to do additional study and learn more. You will be more sensitive to spirits and may encounter them on occasion. You will be wiser and have learned from your mistakes in the past. You will most likely be more creative and receive heavenly inspiration, allowing you to reach your full potential. When you connect with the spirits, you will enjoy a healthy life. You will find the world a more harmonious environment to live in, and you will appreciate your life more. When you conclude your self-journey, don't be unkind; instead, seek to show other friends who have a similar gift to you the path to self-realization.

Anahata is the Heart Chakra.

Though you may believe the heart chakra is located over your heart, it is more central, in the center of your chest, and line with your spine. Anahata means "unbeaten" or "unstruck," which may seem odd given that the heart chakra deals with unbeatable or endless love. It is related to the element air, which symbolizes freedom and expansion.

As one might expect, this chakra is related to giving and receiving love, both essential for our pleasure and well-being. It is the love we display in our relationships and the love we show ourselves. This chakra is linked to the circulatory system, the upper back, the thymus glands (the immune system), and skin, hands, and touch sensations. It is also linked to our lungs due to the element of air.

Surprisingly, ancient yogis believe that the heart chakra has a frequency of 639 Hz, associated with love and healing. Chakras below the heart have a lower frequency because they are connected to our physical selves, but they have a higher frequency because we connect to our higher selves.

The heart chakra sign is a green lotus with 12 petals and two triangles inside that overlap to form a hexagon. The hexagon symbolizes the union of male and feminine forces. Each petal also signifies traits that might obstruct energy flow.

Lust

Fraud

Indecision

Repentance

Hope

Anxiety

Longing

Impartiality

Arrogance

Incompetence

Discrimination

Defiance

Others say that each petal symbolizes the purity of the heart. These are some examples:

Love

Harmony

Empathy

Understanding

Purity

Clarity

Unity in Compassion

Forgiveness

Kindness

Peace and Happiness

How to Spot a Blocked Heart Chakra

Poor circulation and recurrent colds, flu, and infections. When the chakra is blocked, bodily problems such as high or low blood pressure, heart discomfort, or asthma become more acute.

The emotional consequences of an underactive heart chakra are numerous. Once again, the severity of your symptoms can reflect how underactive or even blocked the chakra is. You may have low self-esteem, be shy, or be utterly antisocial to the point of pushing those who care about you away. It is typical to bottle up emotions, which just intensifies them. Some people will put on a tough, brave exterior when extremely weak. Relationships will struggle, perhaps due to a lack of trust, a fear of rejection, a fear of commitment, or holding grudges. Your heart chakra is most likely obstructed if you cannot let go of a prior relationship. If you can't get out of a poisonous relationship, it's even more likely to be prevented.

An overactive heart chakra is characterized by a desire to please others to the point of sacrificing your own needs and well-being for the benefit of others. You may be excessively empathic and overly reliant on others, and your relationships will likely lack healthy limits.

The most powerful feeling you will get when your heart chakra is balanced is unconditional love. When you look at the 12 attributes linked with lotus petals, you get a complete picture of how a balanced heart chakra feels.

How to Heal Your Heart Chakra and Accept Love

Like any other form of physical activity, yoga is essential for heart health. Cardiologist Dr. Helene Glassberg says yoga can enhance cholesterol and blood sugar levels, relax the arteries, and lower blood pressure (Penn Medicine, 2016). Some yoga poses can help you balance your heart chakra while working out.

As you inhale, lift your head, torso, arms, and legs off the ground. Maintain a forward look and a neutral neck position.

Lift your legs and chest as high as possible using your glutes, hamstrings, and lower back muscles. To stretch your lower back, press your pubic bone into the ground.

Hold the stance for 5-10 breaths, then exhale to release.

Repeat the stance 2-3 times more, taking breaks as needed.

Arms rest next to your body, palms facing down.

With your palms facing down and your elbows curled in towards your sides, slide your hands beneath your buttocks.

Press down through your elbows and forearms as you inhale, lifting your chest and head off the ground. Tilt your head back and place your crown on the ground.

Maintain active legs and feet by pressing down through your thighs and the tops of your feet.

Vrksasana (Tree Pose)

Stand at the top of your mat, feet together, and arms beside your body, palms facing forward.

Avoid putting your foot on your knee.

Find a focus point before you to keep your equilibrium and fix your sight on it.

Bring your hands together in front of your heart, palms facing each other. You can also stretch your arms above your head with your palms facing each other.

Maintain a long spine and relaxed shoulders.

Reverse the stance, balancing your right foot and placing your left foot on your right inner thigh.

Solar Plexus Chakra is the third chakra.

This chakra translates straight to "lustrous gem," it is interesting to note that it is the chakra from which your self-belief, confidence, and personal power are produced. If you have been in a position unsuitable for you or had a gut feeling that things would work out, you have tapped into the solar plexus chakra. This is indeed your personal power or solar plexus at work. This confidence can be felt physically within your body or "gut."

This chakra is yellow and is found in the center of the belly button, extending to the breastbone or the crossing point of the two ribs set in the center of your chest. This chakra is associated with a strong sense of wisdom, personal authority, and a decided approach to life when it is balanced. Furthermore, this chakra has been dubbed the warrior chakra since its fundamental feeling is similar to that of a warrior before engaging in difficult combat. Certainly, this warrior has the confidence to win the battle and the intelligence to recognize the truth for which he or she is fighting.

When we are hyperactive, the power we have over our own lives tends to infiltrate the lives of those around us. When too stimulated, one may be extremely fast to respond to anger and have an overpowering urge to control or "micromanage" others around them. Feelings of greed and a lack of empathy are additional signs that this chakra is overactive. Regarding physical symptoms, one may experience digestive problems or persistent imbalances inside internal organs such as the liver and appendix.

This third chakra can be balanced by opening one's heart to feelings of compassion and love. You might want to try sending compassion and love to everyone. Realign your power and start seeing yourself as a beacon of compassion, empathy, and, most importantly, love.

With an underactive third chakra, we may feel our authority has been stolen. This decreased energy level in the third chakra is generally accompanied by visible symptoms such as shyness, timidity, and neediness. However, you can efficiently activate this chakra by merely thinking about some of your innate talents. We all have special talents, abilities, and skills. Making a list can instill and improve your confidence, power, and wisdom. Believing in one's natural talents and gifts causes one's stomach to vibrate and feel alive. You may strengthen this natural feeling by creating affirmations confirming your abilities and increasing your confidence when needed.

8th Chapter

Conclusion and Next Steps

In this last Chapter, we will reflect on our chakra journey, analyzing the important concepts, practices, and insights we received along the way. We will integrate each chakra's wisdom and healing energies, recognizing the significant impact they may have on our bodily, emotional, and spiritual well-being. This Chapter summarizes the book, providing advice on continuing to work with the chakras and keeping balance and harmony in our lives.

The Chakra Journey in Review:

Take a minute to pause and reflect on your remarkable journey. Remember your experiences, problems, and breakthroughs while exploring each chakra. Remember that working with the chakras is a cyclical and ongoing process of self-discovery and growth. Accept the wisdom and healing you've received while recognizing the unique insights and gifts that each chakra has provided.

Recognizing the Chakras' Interconnectedness:

Recognize the interconnectivity of the chakras as you reflect on your journey. Each energy center impacts and supports the others, establishing a comprehensive energy flow system within your being. Understand that an imbalance in one chakra can affect the entire system and that repairing and balancing one chakra can positively impact the others. Accept the fact that nurturing all of the chakras is necessary for overall well-being and spiritual growth.

The Value of Consistent Practice:

The chakra journey is not a destination but rather a continuing practice. Integration of chakra wisdom and healing necessitates continual work and dedication. Incorporate your new techniques and insights into your daily life. Make deliberate decisions that promote your physical, emotional, and spiritual well-being. Develop a way of living that nourishes and balances your chakras, allowing their energies to flow harmoniously.

Keeping the Chakras in Balance:

Listen to your body, emotions, and intuition to balance your chakras. Maintain your awareness of subtle energetic shifts inside yourself, noting any indicators of imbalance or obstacles. Check in with each chakra regularly, checking its vitality and treating any issues that may arise. Trust your inner guidance to restore harmony and balance, and use the practices that resonate with you.

Continued Self-Discovery and Healing:

The chakra path invites deep self-exploration and healing. Recognize that healing is a continuous process that necessitates patience, kindness, and self-love. Allow yourself to investigate any unresolved emotions, limiting beliefs, or patterns that may be stored in your energy centers. Accept practices like journaling, therapy, energy healing, and other therapies to help you recover. Remember that when you recover, you make room for greater harmony with your real essence.

Spirituality and Consciousness Expansion:

The chakra trip also provides a portal to higher consciousness and spiritual development. You open yourself to higher levels of existence, profound spiritual connection, and the unfolding of your true potential as you cultivate awareness and balance within each chakra. Embrace spiritual-connection-deepening techniques such as meditation, prayer, contemplation, and connection with nature.

A Chakra-Centric Way of Life:

Incorporate chakra wisdom into all facets of your life. Adopt a chakra-centric way of life by matching your thoughts, words, actions, and decisions with the energy and attributes of each chakra. In all you do, cultivate love, creativity, personal power, compassion, true expression, intuition, spiritual connection, and togetherness. Remember that living by the chakras improves your health and adds to our planet's collective consciousness and overall healing.

As we near the completion of this transforming trip through the chakras, it is vital to acknowledge the growth, healing, and self-discovery that has occurred. The chakra investigation has given us a profound insight into the energy parts of our being and their enormous impact on our well-being.

We have delved into the traits and attributes of each chakra along this trip, noting their interconnectivity and the need to preserve balance and harmony within the system. We've learned to listen to our bodies, emotions,' and intuition's whispers, knowing that these are powerful markers of the status of our energy centers.

We have awakened the dormant energy within each chakra by engaging in the practices, meditations, and self-reflection exercises, allowing it to flow freely and unobstructedly. We have seen the amazing transformation when we connect ourselves with the chakras' wisdom and healing energies.

However, realizing that the chakra journey is a never-ending process of self-discovery, healing, and progress is critical. The lessons and insights obtained from this voyage are not intended to be contained within the pages of this book but rather to be integrated into our daily lives.

To live a chakra-centered life, we must incorporate the principles and attributes of each chakra into our thoughts, words, actions, and decisions. It entails nurturing love, creativity, personal power, compassion, authenticity, intuition, spiritual connection, and oneness in all our lives. It entails acknowledging our connectivity with all beings and the larger universe.

We must remain open to new experiences and knowledge as we progress along our spiritual path. The chakras are a huge and fascinating subject always being explored and discovered. Allow your curiosity to guide you to new ideas, practices, and therapies that resonate with your soul's journey.

The chakras function as guides and allies on this journey, reminding us of our inherent wisdom and potential. Believe in your intuition and the spiritual direction that comes through you.

May the chakras' wisdom and healing energies illuminate your path, assisting you in your pursuit of completeness, balance, and spiritual progress.Honor the unique properties and vibrations of each energy center within you by embracing the holy dance of the chakras. As you progress, absorb your teachings and incorporate chakra wisdom into your daily life. Allow the chakras' radiant light to guide you to a life of profound alignment, purpose, and joy. Accept the endless possibilities inside you and shine brightly for the benefit of yourself and all beings.

May your chakra path be one of profound self-discovery, healing, and spiritual transformation. Honor the divine light within you by embracing the beauty of your chakra system. You are a luminous creature of love and consciousness intertwined with reality's vast and magnificent tapestry.

May you continue your journey of waking, led by the chakras' wisdom and the limitless potential inside your heart and soul. Trust the trip, for through the chakra investigation; we get to know ourselves and discover our true essence as creatures of light and love.

May you always be in tune with your chakras, and may they act as a beacon of light, directing you to a life full of joy, purpose, and deep spiritual connection. Accept the chakras as a lifetime companion on your path to self-awareness, and may they bring you closer to the truth of who you are.

Awakened.

Chakras and Kundalini

The chakra system gives an excellent framework for comprehending Kundalini. Because the Kundalini is not visible and is solely represented by the symbol of a rising snake, it may be difficult to comprehend how inner movement, healing, and divinity truly occur for you, your healing, and your body. Let's start with your comprehension; I'm convinced you can sort this out. Consider the seven unique "centers" of vital energy that run up your spine. Energy is transmitted from one point to another at each hub; however, congestion can occur. Following a traumatic experience or an argument, some centers may completely shut down, while others may begin channeling energy in the wrong direction, badly affecting the entire system. Those facilities do not always operate at top performance, and this can be due to something as simple as a poor day or a misplaced personality trait.

Consider connecting these seven energy centers to the seven glands that maintain your body (and you) in top shape. Your chakras represent these points. Everything I've described is a genuine possibility, and the worst-case scenario is not ruled out. The Kundalini is rising here. When the time arrives for you to begin your spiritual awakening, the concerns you've been avoiding will become significantly more serious. Their energy will be embedded in your chakras, and it will be up to you to extract the toxins. Your chakras are the seven energy hubs connected with your glands, and we may go over each in depth to help you understand them better. The seven "energy wheels," or chakras, are linked to many things, such as specific colors, body parts, healing energies, etc.

The base chakra is the first chakra we'll look at. Kundalini and Shakti are said to be in harmony. Muladhara, also known as the root chakra, influences your sense of survival, stability, safety, sexuality, and grounding. This chakra is also related to restoring health to the reproductive system, lower extremities, and feet, which governs aspects of your life such as innovation, community, trust, pleasure, and movement. This chakra can heal the digestive tract, the womb, and the elimination system.

Between the diaphragm and the base of the sternum. Which governs our self-esteem, aggressiveness, dominance, need for control, truthfulness, and bravery. Furthermore, this chakra is useful for healing digestive, nervous, and self-esteem issues and toxin clearance.

The fourth chakra, sometimes known as the heart chakra, is located in the center of the chest, as the name suggests. It is related to the color green and the emotions of love, compassion, joy, interpersonal warmth, altruism, and family or relationship; it is also known as Anahata. Furthermore, focusing on this chakra can help with respiratory, circulatory, and skeletal system issues. As you may expect, the fifth chakra is located in the throat. It is blue and also known as Vishuddha. Communication, vocalization, honesty, sharing, support, and hygiene are affected. Its therapeutic scope includes the respiratory, skeletal, and digestive systems.

This chakra, also known as Ajna, is related to the color blue and significantly impacts your capacity for insight, intuition, guidance, reality perception, manifestation, and state of mind. This chakra can also heal the eyes, mind, brain, skin, and ears. Positioned at the top of the head.Sahasrara is its name, and the color associated with it is a magnificent shade of purple. The sacral chakra influences a person's psychic abilities, spirituality, connection to divinity, sense of purpose and mission, life direction, and awareness of cosmic reality. Focusing on this chakra can help with brain, skin, and hair growth issues.

When all seven chakras are spinning freely, and without interference, your Kundalini will naturally ascend toward the happiness it sees above. The ultimate goal in preparing for kundalini awakening is to clear, open, and align the chakras. If you can encourage Kundalini to move as effortlessly as possible, it will demonstrate how intelligent he is. If you're having difficulty with these chakras due to obstacles or energetic reversals, you may notice that your problems take this form. Root chakra blockages can manifest as low vitality, general fear, constant exhaustion, an identity crisis, a sense of disconnection from the world, anorexia, bulimia, an inability to maintain a healthy diet, overt materialism, difficulty saving money, chronic health issues, or any combination of these.

When the energy in the sacral chakra is blocked or reversed, it can manifest as a lack of creativity, inspiration, low or no motivation, low or no sexual appetite, feelings of unimportance, feeling unloved, feeling outcast, an inability to care for oneself, or persistent and recurring problems in one's closest relationships. When one has an identity crisis, a lack of self-esteem or self-worth, digestive problems, food intolerances, a lack of willpower, chronic fatigue, nausea, anxiety, a liver disorder or disease, frequent infections, a lack of core strength, a lack of overall strength, persistent depression with little release, a sense of betrayal, rejection, or replacement, or an abundance of energy, the solar plexus chakra can become blocked.

Inability to love oneself or others put others first, forgive a problematic ex, let go of grudges, trust others, express one's emotions, make and keep friends, commit, delay gratification, be socially anxious or intensely shy, procrastinate, and feel intense anxiety are all symptoms of a blocked or reversed heart chakra. A blocked throat chakra can cause oversharing, inability to speak the truth, difficulty communicating, laryngitis, sore throats, difficulty breathing or communicating, asthma, anemia, constant fatigue, difficulty finding the right words, paralyzing fear of being misunderstood, public-speaking anxiety, occasional intense dizziness, verbal submissiveness, verbal dominance, and conflict avoidance.

A lack of motivation in life, a sense of stagnation or boredom, physical ailments such as headaches, insomnia, eye or vision problems, depression, high blood pressure, an inability to recall dreams, disturbing flashbacks, a lack of openness, paranoia, a history of mental disorders or addiction, a lack of connection to the natural world or to other people, cynicism, constant irritation, or an inability to contrive Feelings of greed, intense depression, a need to dominate others, self-destructive behaviors, a history of addiction or other destructive behaviors, detachment from the physical plane, an inability to make even the most basic decisions, chronic fatigue, excruciating headaches, hair loss, anemia, brain fog, poor mental function, a lack of intellectual abilities, or a sense of not being worthy of divinity, god, or creation can all be manifestations of crown chakra blockages.

Chakra of the Soul Star

The location is six inches above the head.
Description
The soul star chakra is physically located opposite your earth star chakra. It extends from your crown chakra in the same way that your earth star chakra extends from your root chakra. The soul star chakra is associated with your higher self, the center of your existence that endures reincarnations. In fact, many people attempt to discover their former lives through the soul star chakra. Past lifetimes are also known as "Akashic records" and can be used to acquire profound insight into the nature of your soul. We can carry so much from

previous lives that it can substantially influence our fears and talents in this one. Discovering past life events can be just as insightful as discovering childhood trauma—it can provide a lot of insight into who you are today. Some individuals believe that this chakra assists them in connecting with their psychic side. Many people will utilize crystals to more effectively activate this chakra by holding them in the spot above their heads where the soul star chakra is located. Those who have successfully awakened their soul star chakra may experience a higher plane of reality and a stronger relationship with supernatural entities.

Chakra Universale

Description: Location: 12 inches above the skull

The universal chakra is located right above the soul star chakra. The universal chakra is directly related to the oneness of being that we discussed in our Buddhism section. The universal chakra's power will make the universe's fundamental energy available to you. This chakra connects you to the unconditional love and intrinsic connection that flows through the center of our universe. The universal chakra also does not recognize time, thus by opening it, you can free yourself from the oppressive shackles of linear time in exchange for something more eternal. Crystals and crown-focused meditation can help you awaken this chakra and begin dwelling amid the cosmic realities of the great beyond.

Galactic Chakra Location: 2 to 15 feet above the head Description

The placement of the galactic chakra certainly lives up to its name, as it is the highest of the chakras we've seen thus far. This chakra is further away from your body, therefore your body's energy has less of an influence on it, but it doesn't make it any less significant. This chakra enables you to connect with the intergalactic possibilities that exist in the universe. Some refer to the galactic chakra as the "prophecy chakra." It earned this reputation because it aids in divination and fortune-telling. Many skilled psychics will link with those future-connected energies in the universe by tapping into their own cosmic chakras. This chakra, however, helps with more than simply the future; it also aids in the discovery of hidden meanings and deeper truths. Psychics will also invoke their cosmic chakra to assist them see beyond the clutter of daily life to the things that have yet to be disclosed. If you wish to have more insight into the future, or perhaps reach psychic levels, you must actively connect with your galactic chakra.

Location of the Divine Chakra: Above the cosmic chakra to infinity.

Description

The divine chakra is the highest on this list and, indeed, the highest chakra in the entire chakra system. This chakra begins where your galactic chakra ends, enabling you in connecting with powerful eternal forces. The divine chakra connects you to the ultimate form of knowledge and allows you to genuinely climb to the highest point in the cosmos. You have completed your spiritual path and finally grasp the oneness of everything. Those who have successfully linked with their divine chakra are among the most serene and calm individuals you will ever meet. They appear to take everything in stride, as nothing appears to affect them at their core. You will live a life full of superior wisdom and spiritual direction if you balance your heavenly chakra.

I mentioned that I enjoy watching motivating speeches on YouTube, but discover something that works for you. Make a playlist of motivational music, read motivational quotes, watch motivational movies, or speak with a friend or family member. Simply find a means to get motivated from somewhere else so that the responsibility of motivation is not constantly on you when you are unable to do so yourself. Motivation, like a muscle, grows stronger with usage. Most people are unable to perform a pull-up on their own. They must progress to the point where they can accomplish it without assistance. Motivation operates in the same manner. You will make it.

In this chapter, we looked at some strategies for finding and maintaining motivation, particularly while dealing with stress, anxiety, or depression. The first topic we discussed was the need of giving yourself some leeway when beginning an exercise program. Following that, we discussed why it is necessary to start small rather than diving into the deep end of the pool before we are ready. I mentioned how inspiring it might be to begin your exercise regimen with something you currently enjoy. We then discussed how focusing on the good aspects of exercise may be a powerful motivation. Finding an exercise buddy was the second strategy we discussed to help encourage you. We discussed forgiving yourself when you don't accomplish your goals in order to avoid sabotaging your motivation in the future. Finally, we discussed finding motivation to allow someone or something else to motivate you so that you don't always have to do it on your own.

Self-Talk That Is Negative

Anxiety can be caused by actual occurrences (for example, you're concerned because you're behind on your payments) or inaccurate thinking (you tell yourself you're reckless and will certainly fall behind on your bills, even if you haven't done so up to this point). Negative self-talk helps with both types of anxiety. Still, it's especially harmful with the second: A person has experienced or is anticipating an event and is speaking harshly to herself about it. As a result, the situation worsens. Self-talk—what you say to yourself and the "tapes" of conversations or thoughts you play in your head—can sometimes mean the difference between anxiety diminishing or increasing in severity.

We'll look at self-talk in further depth and see how it may transform from an enemy to a valuable friend.

You and Your Inner Dialogue

You talked to yourself as you walked out your front door this morning. You probably asked yourself these questions mentally, without even thinking about it:

- "Do I have my keys?"
- "Which corner does the bus stop on, was it this one or that one?"
- "How much money do I need for the bus and for lunch today?"

Along with these questions, you've probably asked some about the future, such as, "Do I have enough money in my savings account to take that trip to Florida?" You most likely also reminded yourself of what you needed to do today and made some observations about your life and the people in it:

- "I need to turn in that insurance form by Friday." I'll keep it somewhere so I don't forget to send it on time."
- "I'm afraid I can't attend that job interview right now." I'm sick with a cold and won't be confident."
- "My parents are such jerks—everyone else is allowed to go out late on Friday nights except me." "I despise my life."

The persistent voice chatters away to you all day, giving you the play-by-play of your existence.

Negative Self-Talk Is Your Enemy

The real issue arises when your self-talk robs you of changes or forces you to take behaviors that harm your health. When you find yourself participating in self-defeating behavior, such as lashing out in anger at someone or simply feeling unhappy, depressed, and lacking confidence, this is when it is time to seek help. Self-talk drains you and tells you how horrible things are. After hearing it enough times, you begin to believe it. Self-talk can become so habitual that you don't even realize it's there. You may not think of it as talking to yourself but as observing what is happening around you. Negative self-talk is a frequent visitor for many people, but it is not your friend. It is not assisting you in any manner.

That is the unfortunate news. The good news is that you can adjust your inner dialogue. It is not fixed and unchangeable. Self-talk, especially positive self-talk, can be a valuable ally in the fight against anxiety. To change a negative into a positive, remember what you tell yourself when things aren't going well. What thoughts come to mind when you are confronted with a challenging situation? Bring your self-talk to the surface so you can notice it and work with it more effectively.

For example, perhaps you are having difficulty at work. "I will never be able to please this boss," your negative self-talk script says. He doesn't appreciate me no matter how hard I work." Perhaps you are experiencing negativity in your connections. "How did I decide to marry this person?" you wonder. "I despise her." She's not even my style. I despise sitting at the dinner table with her every night. What happened to my high school sweetheart? We'd be overjoyed right now."

This is how negative self-talk takes over. But consider what would happen if you reversed this. Suppose you thought to yourself, "Wow! I'm extremely fortunate to be married to such a beautiful person! I cherish our time together. We do have some differences, but we can work on them, and compared to the emotional and other benefits I get from our marriage, that's a tiny price to pay." Every time you saw your spouse, you'd get a rush of happiness. Spending time with her or him would be pleasurable. When positive self-talk takes hold, this is what can happen.

We'll go over this chakra in great detail in the following chapter, so I'll move on to the final chakra in this chapter.

The Crown Chakra is known as Sahasrara.

If the sixth chakra is all about comprehending the fundamental nature of reality, the seventh—and final—chakra is all about experiencing joy like you've never experienced before. This chakra is physically positioned at the top of the head, commonly known as the crown. This chakra is represented as a thousand-petaled lotus. No element represents the topmost chakra. When it comes to colors, some individuals believe violet can represent it. Most people, however, think that this chakra is symbolized by the color white, which represents the mixture of all the rainbow colors, referring to the chakra's universal vitality.

Because this chakra is linked to all the other chakras, it can affect every aspect of our body. It directly impacts our head and spinal system because it is placed on the top of the head. This chakra is associated with unconditional joy—even ecstasy—emotionally. In this moment, one is blissfully united with the Higher Consciousness.

While this chakra is also known as the chakra of enlightenment, "enlightenment" in this context refers to the ability to experience a state fully beyond the human. This is also why no path connects the sixth and seventh chakras. In other words, you can do nothing to stimulate the activation of this chakra. This stage, if anything, demands an entire surrender to the infinite—almost like the ability to enter into an unending dance with the unknowable.

When this chakra is obstructed, we may have headaches and hearing and visual issues. At the same time, we may become vividly aware of the world's conflicts. Instead of welcoming everything with open arms, we may become cautious and narrow-minded. We may grow unduly connected to our physical world rather than yielding to the unknown.

To be honest, this chakra has no "material" counterpart, but we can understand it through certain notions. For example, the crescent moon visible on Shiva's head represents this state. This crescent moon represents the happiness and intoxication we experience in this state. The key goal for those lucky enough to experience this condition is to avoid becoming so engrossed in it that physical existence becomes impossible.

Before we proceed to the next chapter, while the fundamental concepts stay the same, everyone's route is unique. A key component of a spiritual journey is determining what the journey means to us and gaining a greater understanding of ourselves. You can make this journey your own if you keep that in mind.

Another consideration is that your chakra awakening path may not be linear. Of course, we must first acquire a certain level of alignment before moving on to the higher chakras. However, the voyage itself may take an unconventional path. Also, just because your chakra has been aligned once does not mean it cannot be obstructed again in the future. Indeed, depending on our physical, mental, and emotional states, we may need to start working on our foundations occasionally. This is not to say that the progress we've made thus far on the voyage is insignificant. All it means is that we must change our perspective on spiritual advancement. Even when it appears that we are beginning from scratch or regressing, we are coming closer to the most true version of ourselves—which makes this trip worthwhile.

The following chapter will review the third eye chakra in depth.

The third eye chakra is linked to "light." This deserves some clarity. Because this chakra is related to "insight," the concept of vision is crucial here. The two "physical" eyes observe the tangible world, but the third eye allows us to see beyond the material plane. Even now, we can only see something if it interacts with light. Light represents profound wisdom, clarity, and insight in spiritual terms.

When we consider light as an element, it moves quicker than sound. Furthermore, light has an intriguing relationship with the universe. For example, sunlight takes around eight minutes to reach the Earth. Similarly, when we get light from various stars in the universe, we view them not as they are now but as they were when lighted by this light. When we compare it to the third eye chakra, we discover that we have the power to see not only in the past or future but also between dimensions.

Another related school of thought holds that no element is associated with this chakra because it does not interact with anything on this plane of existence. This is why the name Avyakta is applied to this chakra. Avyakta means "that which is without form" or "that which cannot be expressed."

Mudra Related to the Third Eye Chakra

In ancient religions such as Hinduism, Buddhism, and Jainism, Mudras are important in helping us regulate our prana. They are frequently used in conjunction with meditation and yoga.

While mudras can encompass our complete body, most are hasta mudras or hand movements. Mudras are used for a variety of purposes. These can aid in enhancing our bodily, emotional, and spiritual processes. Mudras are also an important element of our spiritual enlightenment.

The hakini mudra is the mudra linked with the third eye chakra. Hakini means "power" or "rule" in Sanskrit and is tied to the Hindu goddess Hakini. Goddess Hakini represents both hemispheres of the brain and is associated with inner understanding, intuition, and imagination, all of which are elements of the third eye chakra.

SWADHISTHANA CHAKRA ADVANCED HEALING AND UNBLOCKING S it in a comfortable position. Cross your legs so that one rests on top of the other.

(A 10-second pause)

You can hold your hands in Chin mudra or Dhyana mudra. The palms of your hands are softly placed on your knees in Chin. The fingers and palms should be relaxed.

(A 5-second pause)

The palms of your hands are placed on your lap in Dhyana mudra. The left palm rests on the right. Dhyana mudra aids in the development of concentration. Dhyana is the Sanskrit word for concentration. The left hand in Dhyana mudra represents the illusionary or material world. The spiritual world is represented by the right hand resting on the left.

(A 5-second pause)

Bring your attention back to your body. You are sitting with your back straight. Your back is straight. Your head is parallel to your spine.

(Pause for 5 seconds) Now, pay attention to your breathing. Your breath must come from your gut. Feel your belly's expansion when inhaling and your belly's contraction when exhaling. Do not try to hold your breath. With each breath, feel your mind and body relax. For another minute, keep your eyes on your breath.

(One minute pause)

The Swadhisthana chakra unblocking and balancing practice begins.

Gently remind yourself that you are balancing and repairing the Swadhisthana chakra. Behind the genitals is the Swadhisthana chakra. Energy manifests as sexual energy in the sacral chakra, also known as the Swadhisthana chakra. Consider your genital area in your mind's eye. Take note of the orange light that has engulfed the surroundings.

(A 10-second pause)

Allow the orange warmth to permeate your thoughts. Continue to visualize this while listening to the guided voice. To increase your creative and sexual instincts, the Swadhisthana chakra must be balanced. Sex and creativity are both primal drives. Through their inherent creativity, humans have been known to create, build, and construct new opportunities, fresh notions, and creative ideas.

The source of this creative desire is the conversion of sexual energy into productive endeavors. Some people allow the sexual drive to become all-powerful and all-encompassing to the detriment of all other useful pursuits.

Such persons have an overactive Swadhisthana chakra, which is imbalanced. An underactive Swadhisthana chakra, on the other hand, results in poor libido and complete indifference to creative endeavors.

The Swadhisthana chakra should ideally be balanced. You should be able to simply segue from sex to creative activity. The Swadhisthana chakra must be balanced through a process.

(A 2-second pause)

You'll now do an activity to balance the Swadhisthana chakra. Visualize your sacral chakra, also known as the Swadhisthana chakra. The area beneath your navel, known as the genitals, is orange. In your mind's eye, the orange appears like a little dot.

(A 10-second pause)

Bring your attention to your thoughts while keeping the orange visualization in your mind. Consider your thoughts to be a movie. Interjecting or interrupting the flow of thought is not permitted. Simply observe objectively. Make yourself an observer or data. The cognitive process is not to be intellectualized.

Your subconscious generates these thoughts. You are the owner of these items. Do not dismiss the ideas. Simply watch them travel across your head like clouds.

Allowing Sensuality to Bring About Authenticity and Emotional Liberation by Accepting Vulnerability

Vulnerability is the doorway to true connection, emotional emancipation, and deep connection. Embracing vulnerability in sensuality allows you to peel aside the layers of safety and masks, revealing your true self to yourself and others. Here are some tips for embracing vulnerability in your sensory exploration:

Build Trust and Safety:

Make your sensual experiences a safe and trusting environment. This may entail establishing clear boundaries, stating your wishes and limits, and ensuring you are safe and comfortable.

Let Go of Shame and Judgment:

Allow society indoctrination and personal prejudices about sensuality to go. Accept that your sensuous nature is lovely, natural, and deserving of celebration. Allow yourself to freely express and experience pleasure by letting go of shame and guilt.

Authentic Communication: Communicate openly and honestly with yourself and any companions with whom you share your sensual journey. Declare your wants, needs, and boundaries, and invite others to do the same. Authentic communication builds trust, strengthens bonds, and promotes mutual respect and understanding.

Self-Exploration and Self-Acceptance: Use sensuality to explore yourself, enabling yourself to fully embrace and accept your desires, fantasies, and individual manifestations of pleasure. Engage in self-pleasure techniques that build self-acceptance and love, embracing your real self and celebrating the diversity of human sensuality.

You can achieve emotional emancipation, sincerity, and genuine connection by accepting vulnerability within sensuality. Vulnerability liberates you from the confines of society's standards and allows you to tap into the raw and real power of your sensual nature.

The disciplines of sensual healing, nourishing the inner child, and embracing vulnerability intersect to produce a transforming emotional release and growth journey in investigating sensuality as a path to healing. These techniques can help you heal from trauma and emotional wounds, nurture your inner child, and access the profound authenticity and vulnerability that sensuality provides. Allow sensuality to be your guide as you begin on an emotional healing and liberation journey, embracing sensuality's transformational ability to awaken your true nature and build a life of profound connection, joy, and emotional well-being.

As a Spiritual Practice, Sensuality

Divine Connection Awakening

When handled with reverence and intention, sensuality can enhance our spiritual connection, ignite our inner flame, and awaken a profound sense of divine presence within us. In this section, we will look at how sensuality can be used as a spiritual practice to delve into the mystical depths of our being and awaken our divine connection.

Sensual Spirituality is the incorporation of sensuality into pre-existing spiritual practices.

Spirituality is frequently associated with transcending the physical sphere; nevertheless, embracing sensuality as a spiritual practice allows us to incorporate the sacred into all aspects of our existence. We build a holistic approach that recognizes our embodied experience by incorporating sensuality into our spiritual practices. Here are several approaches to sensual Spirituality:

Rituals of Mindfulness:

Incorporate sensual components into your established spiritual routines. Use aromatic candles, quiet music, or tactile materials like crystals or feathers to stimulate your senses. Allow yourself to be completely immersed in the sensory experience, increasing your relationship with the divine.

Sensual Movement: Incorporate sensual movement disciplines such as yoga, tai chi, or dance into your spiritual routine. Allow your body to move in a delightful and liberated way, allowing the movement to serve as a prayer and an expression of your divine connection.

Nature Connection:

Engage in sensual and respectful interactions with nature.

Walk barefoot on the land, let the breeze caress your skin, and immerse yourself in the healing waters of rivers or oceans.

Allow nature's sensory gifts to awaken your awareness of the natural world's holiness.

Mindful Eating: Approach your meals mindfully and gratefully. Allow eating to become a sacred connection with the divine, honoring the abundance and sustenance provided for you.

We increase our awareness of the divine presence in every moment and improve our connection with the sacredness of life by incorporating sensuality into our spiritual activities.

FROM SUBTLE TO GROSS, FROM SUBTLE TO GROSS

Truth has been sought for thousands of years and continues to be sought. In this context, truth refers to the Ultimate Truth, the eternal answer to issues. Many anecdotes about this hunt may be found in India. Lord Vishnu is one such narrative. Lord Vishnu's condition was terrible when he left Vaikuntha (his dwelling) and ran out in a state of restlessness.

In this state, he meets NaradaMaharshi on his route, who asks him why he is fleeing. What is the cause of his illness? Lord Vishnu claims he is fleeing because he needs a hiding place. NaradaMaharshi inquires why he wants to flee his Vaikunthdham. Lord Vishnu informs him that man is not enabling him to live in peace anyplace. Man has made me restless by singing and praying in temples from Brahma-muhurta (early morning) to late at night.

Because of this, I went to the Amarnath Himalaya and disguised myself as a Shivling. Humans discovered me and began to worship me. Their worship makes me restless, and now man has grown so powerful that he is approaching Vaikunth directly. That is why I am fleeing to another location to hide so that no one can ever discover me and I may live happily.

After hearing the Lord's predicament, NaradaMaharshi begins to consider how serious the Lord's plight is.

NaradaMaharshi considers how to get God out of this situation. He has an epiphany at that precise time. "Humans have become so intelligent today that they can find you anywhere," he informs God. No matter where you hide on Earth or in the universe, man will find you. But, my Lord, there is a hidden location where humans will never be able to find you."

"That is the only way to avoid detection by humans." Man will look for you everywhere, but he will never be able to locate you in his lifetime. And it's such a mysterious location to live happily."

God is overjoyed and quickly says, "Tell me soon Narada, tell me soon... where is this place?" According to Sage NaradaMaharshi, the location is within the human person.

"What?" God inquires, astonished. "Yes, man will try to find you everywhere," NaradaMaharshi explains. But he will never be able to locate you within himself."

"Man will try to find you in everything in the world... in food, in drink, in sleep, in travel, in name, in glory, in friends, in relationships, in wealth, in splendour, in buildings, in cars, in success, in gardens, at seashores... like this he will try to find you everywhere outside and in everything, but he will never look within."

God rejoices upon hearing this. And God quickly enters the human's thinking.

Man has been striving for truth, solution, peace, happiness, love, and God for thousands of years.

Similarly, the author began his pursuit of truth in his life at the age of 12.

What is the source of the problem? What is the underlying cause of diseases? How do you get rid of fear for good? How do you keep your rage under control? How do you break harmful habits? What is the most effective formula for success? How do I get over my grief?

Many of these questions took 30 years to address. He was always looking since author Mr. Ganesh Karapu's life was filled with physical, mental, financial, and family issues, as if a helpless individual is imprisoned in a marsh.

Because of these challenges, the author's entire life was spent searching for truth rather than enjoying life's pleasures.

Detachment had made him spiritual since childhood because he learned there is no eternal solution to any problem or scenario in the material world.

In our human reality, situations are created and controlled from somewhere else. Its finding transformed him spiritually.

But where should one begin in their search for Spirituality?

It lacked comprehension and direction. However, that universe had to be comprehended and entered. Because that was the only place to look for the truth. After many days of contemplation, he began his search by examining spiritual writings that he came across. Because the country's renowned gurus write spiritual literature in India, they have accumulated all of their knowledge, experiences, discoveries, and many more secrets for the benefit of humanity.

He went ahead with the help of these texts, that is, with the blessings of his ancestors. He discovered the secret that our body is the entryway to the spiritual world by studying several writings such as the Ramayana, Mahabharata, Bhagwat, Vedas, Shastras, and Bhagavad Gita. To comprehend the universe's mysteries. Because the mysteries of the universe are buried in the body, our forefathers stated that the universe is in the body itself (pind me bramhandhain). The more he realized this, the more devoted he grew to contemplation, experimenting with various meditation techniques.

Once this strategy was learned, solving every life problem became incredibly simple. Previously, years of hard work and lengthy waiting did not solve problems. In reality, many problems appeared to have little possibility of being solved. However, he realized that the voyage into the inner world solves all of your issues.

Imbalances in the Throat Chakra (Vishuddha): The throat chakra governs communication, self-expression, and honesty. Throat chakra imbalances can emerge as:

Physical symptoms include a sore throat, thyroid problems, neck and shoulder pain, and dental troubles.

Difficulty expressing oneself or speaking up, dread of public speaking, feeling unheard or misunderstood, or excessive talking or dominating conversations are all emotional and behavioral tendencies.

Difficulties stating one's truth or standing up for oneself.

Imbalances in the Third Eye Chakra (Ajna): The third eye chakra is related to intuition, perception, and inner wisdom. Third-eye chakra imbalances might emerge as:

Headaches, migraines, eye problems, sinus issues, or sleep disturbances are all examples of physical symptoms.

Difficulty accessing intuition or inner direction, feeling disconnected from one's purpose or intuition, an overreliance on logic or external validation, or being unduly judgmental or dismissive of intuition and spiritual experiences are all emotional and behavioral tendencies.

Uncertainty or trouble making decisions. Imbalances in the Crown Chakra (Sahasrara): The crown chakra signifies our connection to divine consciousness and spiritual awakening. Crown chakra imbalances can emerge as:

Some physical symptoms include chronic weariness, sensitivity to light or sound, neurological diseases, or problems with the upper skull or brain.

Disconnection from Spirituality or higher realms, a lack of purpose or direction, skepticism or cynicism towards spiritual concepts, or a rigid attachment to religious or spiritual dogma.Difficulty accessing higher states of consciousness or experiencing spiritual connection.

Recognizing chakra imbalances is critical to recognizing the parts of our lives that may require healing and repair. We can acquire insights into the precise imbalances we may be experiencing by paying attention to the physical, emotional, and spiritual indications and symptoms connected with each chakra.

It is critical to remember that chakra imbalances are interrelated and that an imbalance in one chakra can affect the others. As a result, a comprehensive approach to chakra healing is required, addressing all areas of imbalance.

The next chapters will examine techniques, exercises, and meditations for healing and balancing each chakra, restoring energy flow, and fostering holistic well-being. We can start on a revolutionary journey of self-discovery, healing, and personal growth by being aware of and fixing imbalances in our chakras.

Effects of Chakra Blockage or Imbalance

Block or misaligned chakras can have serious consequences for our bodily, emotional, and spiritual well-being. When the flow of energy within our chakras is obstructed or interrupted, it can manifest in various ways, affecting numerous aspects of our lives. In this chapter, we will look at the impacts of blocked or imbalanced chakras, how they develop, and the ramifications for our overall health and vitality. Understanding these consequences is critical for appreciating the significance of chakra healing.

Physical repercussions: Chakras that are blocked or imbalanced can have palpable repercussions on our physical bodies. Each chakra is related to certain organs, glands, and body systems, and when energy flow is interrupted, physical symptoms and diseases can occur. Chronic pain or discomfort in the corresponding places of the body are some of the main physical symptoms of blocked or unbalanced chakras.

Immune system weakness and vulnerability to illness or disease.

Stomachaches, indigestion, or irritable bowel syndrome are examples of digestive problems.

Hormonal imbalances and reproductive problems are common.

Respiratory issues, such as asthma or Difficulty breathing.

Chronic tiredness, fatigue, or a lack of energy.

Emotional and psychological effects: Chakras that are blocked or imbalanced can substantially impact our emotional and psychological well-being. Each chakra is associated with different emotional aspects, and when the energy within the chakra becomes stagnant or excessive, it can affect our emotional state and mental processes. The emotional and psychological impacts of chakra blockages or imbalances may include:

Anxiety, fear, or an overall feeling of dread.

Depression, melancholy, or a lack of motivation are all symptoms.

Emotional instability or mood swings.

The inability to articulate feelings or communicate requirements.

Self-esteem, self-worth, or self-confidence issues.

Anger, frustration, or annoyance that is irrational or excessive.

Indecisiveness, lack of clarity, or a sense of being alienated from oneself.

Problems with Relationships and Communication:

Chakra blockages or imbalances can also impact our relationships and communication with others. The throat chakra, in particular, is critical to our ability to express ourselves authentically and form healthy connections. When these chakras are blocked or imbalanced, it can result in Difficulty in building intimate relationships or deep connections.

Inadequate communication and misreading of intentions.

Inability to clearly explain wants, desires, or boundaries.

Isolation or feeling disconnected from others.

Difficulties are listening attentively or empathizing with others.

What Is Kundalini and What Does It Awaken?

The previous chapter gave you a taste of what Kundalini Awakening can be. This chapter is solely dedicated to the Kundalini Awakening. You will discover what it is, how to awaken it (both spontaneously and purposefully), the symptoms you are likely to experience, and how it feels.

To summarize, Kundalini is the female creative energy that lies dormant (in the shape of a coiled serpent) at the base of each of our spines. However, there is no empirical evidence that this snake-like element exists in our bodies. It is a subtle energy form you can awaken and recognize when you experience its strength.

Like prana and the nadis or channels through which it flows, Kundalini is invisible to the naked eye but may be felt and experienced when it is active. Other parts of our non-physical self are contained in this subtle form of energy, such as energetic imprints, inherent and acquired patterns of energies, and emotional imprints. Kundalini is the location of our life experiences, including those formed by our family, culture, and society (together known in Sanskrit as "samskara").

Interestingly, although the energy housed in our Kundalini may appear metaphorical or even metaphysical to novices, it is not. Kundalini is subtle but exists, and many of us can activate and wake it through various ways, such as meditation, yoga, and others.

The Kundalini energy can be felt like you can feel your skin or see something colorful through your eyes. In the awakened state, you can feel Kundalini energy dancing up and down your spine and the nadis in your body. You can feel the disintegration of any energy barriers in your body as it moves freely. As the many energy blocks created throughout time are freed, your insight into long-held ideas improves, and you can see things more clearly.

Most experts will concur that awakening the Kundalini without guru supervision can be hazardous to you and those around you. Kundalini awakening can occur as a result of trauma, a near-death experience, a crippling sickness, dreams, drug addiction, and abuse, or even having intercourse with a partner who has an aroused Kundalini. Awakening the Kundalini necessitates unparalleled levels of physical and mental discipline to be prepared to bear the responsibilities that come with the power of awakening the natural Kundalini.

So, what is the point of attempting to activate Kundalini Shakti? The Kundalini eventually returns to God, or the global divine power. It also helps to let go of your ego when you surrender to cosmic divinity. The ultimate goal of Kundalini awakening is self-realization.

Yes, Kundalini awakening may appear to be a bizarre experience that could lead to conditions beyond human control. However, this is only one aspect of the process. Kundalini is, in reality, an organic and intelligent process with a logical ultimate goal.

An awakened Kundalini assists you in untying all emotional and mental knots in your head so that you can see the true purpose of your existence in particular and the Universe in general. Kundalini awakening is the manifestation of Shakti inside you. It also indicates that the route for Shiva to enter you is being cleansed and prepared.

When Shakti's Kundalini awakens, she calls Shiva to come down and meet her, even as she goes up to meet Him. More than attempting to transcend our lives, Kundalini Awakening is an exercise in bringing spirituality into our worldly reality. Kundalini Awakening cleans our body, mind, and soul to become vessels for the global divine power inside us.

Kundalini Awakening is usually regarded as a divine revelation since it is associated with many mystical experiences such as connection with the entire Universe, bliss, gorgeous colors and lights, and perception of beyond-human realms of consciousness. Surprisingly, the Kundalini Awakening is the initial step in a long journey back to your origins. When you reawaken the dormant, sleeping Shakti, the real job begins.

If you have undergone spiritual healing and purification, the Kundalini awakening will be a smooth and not-so-difficult transition. However, if the Shakti awakens before you are ready or if you are in a rush, the experience might be unpleasant.

When the Kundalini awakens, it is analogous to awakening a sleeping giant or giantess. She'll cleanse your body, heart, and mind. However, if you have the Kundalini before dealing with difficulties and other unpleasant areas of your life, the "cleansing" process can be quite painful. As a result, you must not force the Kundalini to awaken. Allow

Her to awaken when She knows you are ready to welcome Her in an active condition.

The purifying process required before awakening Kundalini Shakti can be challenging and powerful. You may need to be hospitalized or perhaps institutionalized since living in the worldly world with a fully awakened Kundalini can be rather unsettling. Your world will never be the same when She awakens.

As a result, if you want to awaken the Kundalini Shakti that is dormant inside you, be sure you fully comprehend its potential significance. Recognize the depth of your ambitions and accept that the road ahead will not be easy. Finally, remind yourself that if you activate the Kundalini, you may wish you hadn't.

Awakening the Kundalini Shakti is about more than only psychic abilities, happiness, and oneness with the Universe. It is also the effort required on the spiritual journey. However, once SHE is awake, she is in command, and you can only do what she tells you to do. So, make your decision after careful consideration.

www.ingramcontent.com/pod-product-compliance
Lightning Source LLC
Chambersburg PA
CBHW052138110526
44591CB00012B/1771